POSITIVE

THINKING

Journal

A 365 Day POSITIVITY Journal

POSITIVE THINKING

Journal

A 365 Day POSITIVITY Journal

Cameon Galli

CORAL GABLES

Book layout: Kim Balacuit
Cover design: Lilia Garvin
Images used under license from Adobe Stock

For permission requests, please contact the publisher at:
Mango Publishing Group
2850 S Douglas Road, 4th Floor
Coral Gables, FL 33134 USA
info@mango.bz

For special orders, quantity sales, course adoptions and corporate sales, please
email the publisher at sales@mango.bz. For trade and wholesale sales, please
contact Ingram Publisher Services at customer.service@ingramcontent.com
or +1.800.509.4887.

Positive Thinking Journal: A 365 Day Positivity Journal for Kids

ISBN: (print) 978-1-64250-705-8
BISAC JNF029060, JUVENILE NONFICTION / Language Arts /
Journal Writing

Printed in the United States of America

THIS JOURNAL BELONGS TO:

_____

IN THE YEAR OF _____

 This is me with three things I'm thankful for!

This journal is all about YOU. It is a safe, creative place for you to write down your thoughts, feelings, and reflections.

There are 365 prompts, one for every day of the year. Set aside a few minutes each day to fill out just one. These prompts will get you thinking about how truly unique you are and how you are making a difference in this world. And writing daily will help you develop a healthy routine of caring for yourself during mindful quiet time.

Reflect on how you turn away from negative thoughts to build positive ones. Your observations will help you see daily opportunities to think positively, help others, extend kindness, and love yourself.

Throughout this journal, you'll occasionally find weekly reflection pages. This is a place for you to review your week while looking for gratitude in all the moments and experiences you have shared.

There are coloring pages with positive sayings sprinkled throughout your journal too. Keep your colored pencils or favorite gel pens stored nearby so that you can indulge in some relaxation, self-care, and positive color therapy.

To stay on track, you'll find 12 monthly calendars for you to fill in the dates. Use these to plan your month, reflect upon your wins of each day, or as a mood tracker. It's your journal, so use it however it feels best for you!

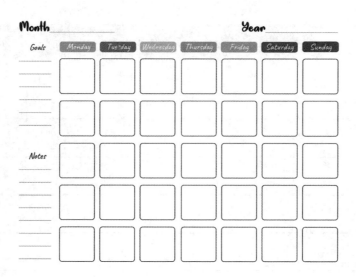

And to top it all off, there's also a gratitude scavenger hunt in the back of this book. Take your time with this activity, and even use the notes section to reflect on your findings.

Have fun within these pages! Grab your favorite pens or pencils and make this a special place for all your thoughts.

Mon — I am unique because:

Tue — 5 things I love about me:

1 _____

2 _____

3 _____

4 _____

5 _____

Wed — My best quality is:

Thu — 3 words that best describe me:

1 _____

2 _____

3 _____

Fri I'm happiest when:

Sat Here's a drawing of me:

Sun I am really good at:

BE YOURSELF;
EVERYONE
ELSE IS
ALREADY TAKEN.

Oscar Wilde, Irish poet

9

Mon

Tue

Wed

Thu

Fri

Sat

Sun

A reflection on my week:

_____

_____

_____

Mon When talking to myself, the words of kindness I use are:

 Tue An accomplishment I am proud of:

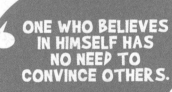 **Wed** When thinking about the future, I most look forward to:

ONE WHO BELIEVES IN HIMSELF HAS NO NEED TO CONVINCE OTHERS.

Laozi, Chinese philosopher

Thu If I were a professional athlete, I would be:

 Fri One time I succeeded when I thought I might fail:

 Sat The part of my school day that I enjoy most is _____ because:

Sun Today I am taking this step toward achieving my goal:

13

Mon Being thankful means:

Tue Someone who I thanked today:

Wed When someone extends kindness to me
when I'm struggling with something, I feel:

KINDNESS IS THE
LANGUAGE WHICH
THE DEAF CAN
HEAR AND THE
BLIND CAN SEE.

Mark Twain,
American writer

Thu A person I am thankful for is
_____ because:

Fri — 3 ways I can show others I'm thankful:

- _____
- _____
- _____

Sat — Something I can do to cheer someone up:

Sun — Today I will write a thank you note to
_____ because:

Month_____

Goals

	Monday	Tuesday	Wednesday
_____			
_____			
_____			
_____			

Notes

_____

_____

_____

_____

_____

Year _____

Thursday	Friday	Saturday	Sunday

Mon Right now I am feeling:

Tue One goal I have for today is:

Wed Today, I am most grateful for
_____ because:

One thing I've been afraid to do is: **Thu**

Fri I am grateful for my family because:

I am proud of myself for: **Sat**

 Sun A memory that makes me smile:

Mon My best friends are:

THERE IS NOTHING ON THIS EARTH MORE TO BE PRIZED THAN TRUE FRIENDSHIP.

St. Thomas Aquinas, Italian philosopher

 Tue Being a good friend means:

Wed My friend that makes me feel most special is _____ because:

Thu Being with my friends makes me feel:

 Fri Important people who I trust:

 Sat What I like most about my best friend is:

Sun Here's a picture about when a friend made my day:

Mon 3 ways that I can show love to people in my life:

1 _____

2 _____

3 _____

Tue The best part about my day was:

Wed What it means to look on the bright side:

Thu 3 things I can say to myself when I start feeling frustrated:

1 _____

2 _____

3 _____

Fri — *I choose to see the good during tough times by:*

KEEP YOUR FACE ALWAYS TOWARD THE SUNSHINE— AND SHADOWS WILL FALL BEHIND YOU.

Walt Whitman, American poet

 Sat — *On a scale of 1–5, my positive thinking today is:*

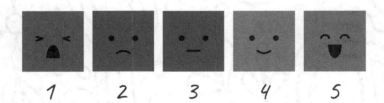

1   2   3   4   5

 Sun — *One time I remained positive in a difficult situation was:*

Mon

Tue

Wed

Thu

Fri

Sat

Sun

A reflection on my week:

_____

_____

_____

Mon

3 things I do to relax:

· _____

· _____

· _____

Tue

I can relax my mind by:

> WE DELIGHT IN THE BEAUTY OF THE BUTTERFLY, BUT RARELY ADMIT THE CHANGES IT HAS GONE THROUGH TO ACHIEVE THAT BEAUTY.
>
> *Maya Angelou, American poet*

Wed

2 things that bring me peace:

1 _____

2 _____

Thu Stretching is a good exercise because:

 Fri Writing in my journal makes me feel:

Sat My favorite thing to do to relax is:

 Sun A special quiet place where I like to retreat is:

Month_____

Goals

	Monday	Tuesday	Wednesday
_____			
_____			
_____			
_____			
_____			

Notes

_____

_____

_____

_____

_____

_____

Year _____

Thursday	Friday	Saturday	Sunday

Mon · I love my family because:

LOVE INSPIRES, ILLUMINATES, DESIGNATES AND LEADS THE WAY.

*Mary Baker Eddy,
American author*

Tue · 3 words my family would use to describe me:

- _____
- _____
- _____

Wed · One thing I've been thinking about, but am not quite ready to talk about yet:

Thu This is why I do (or don't) consider pets to be family members:

Fri One special tradition our family does is:

Sat My most memorable family trip:

Sun Of all my family members, I'm most like:

31

Mon

Tue

Wed

Thu

Fri

Sat

Sun

A reflection on my week:

_____

_____

_____

Mon — 3 things I love most about my life:

- _____
- _____
- _____

Tue — Something beautiful I saw today:

Wed — The best thing that happened today was:

Thu — Being grateful means:

> GRATITUDE TURNS WHAT WE HAVE INTO ENOUGH.
>
> Melody Beattie,
> American author

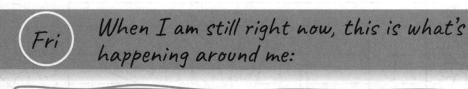

Fri When I am still right now, this is what's happening around me:

Sat I am thankful for school because:

Sun A gift that I am grateful for:

Mon

3 things that always make me smile:

1 _____

2 _____

3 _____

My favorite thing about nature is: **Tue**

Wed My favorite season is _____ because:

By the end of today, I want to feel: **Thu**

Fri Today I am grateful for:

I feel most energized when: **Sat**

Sun My favorite time of day is:

Mon — My body is strong and helps me to:

Tue — I keep my body strong by:

Wed — 3 of my favorite things about my body:

- _____
- _____
- _____

Thu — My body supported me today by:

Fri I fuel my body with healthy foods like:

 Sat My favorite physical feature about myself is:

YOU'RE AMAZING JUST THE WAY YOU ARE.

Bruno Mars, American singer

Sun Today I will do these activities so that I feel healthy and full of energy:

Month_____

Goals

Monday	Tuesday	Wednesday

_____
_____
_____
_____
_____

Notes

_____
_____
_____
_____
_____
_____

Year _____

Thursday	Friday	Saturday	Sunday

Mon The first thing that comes to my mind is:

Something new I've learned this week: **Tue**

 Wed Some may not agree, but I think:

One thing I believe is: **Thu**

Fri One thing I wish I could change is:

I am not afraid to say: **Sat**

 Sun If I found $500, I would:

Mon — My favorite holiday memory is:

Tue — If I could go back in time for one day, I would:

Wed — My happiest memory with friends is:

THE BEST THING ABOUT MEMORIES IS MAKING THEM!
Author unknown

44

Thu My favorite memory at school is:

 Fri The best gift I've ever received is
_____ because:

 Sat When I was little, my favorite activity was:

 Sun My favorite family vacation was:

Mon When I see someone who is sad or hurting, I:

Tue A chore that I like to help with is _____ because:

Wed 3 things I can do to help others today is:

1 _____

2 _____

3 _____

Thu The kindest thing someone has done for me is:

Fri When I help others, I feel:

Sat I can encourage people around me by:

Sun Something I can do to help those who are less fortunate:

AFTER THE VERB 'TO LOVE,' 'TO HELP' IS THE MOST BEAUTIFUL VERB IN THE WORLD.

Bertha von Suttner, Austrian novelist

Mon

Tue

Wed

Thu

Fri

Sat

Sun

A reflection on my week:

_____

_____

_____

Mon My favorite thing to do outdoors is:

IN ALL THINGS OF NATURE THERE IS SOMETHING OF THE MARVELOUS.

*Aristotle,
Greek philosopher*

Tue Here are some drawings of different shapes or animals I found in the clouds:

Wed One thing I think about more than anything else:

Thu My favorite place outside to explore is
_____ because:

 Fri Some things I can do to better protect
our natural world are:

 Sat My favorite thing that lives outside is
_____ because:

 Sun My favorite winter activity is:

Month_____

Goals

	Monday	Tuesday	Wednesday

_____
_____
_____

_____
_____

Notes

_____

_____
_____

_____
_____

Year _____

Thursday	Friday	Saturday	Sunday

Mon Some people whose footsteps I would like to follow are:

Tue Here are some of the craziest ideas I've had for my future:

Wed Today I am going to learn the meaning of two new words:

1 _____

2 _____

Thu Something I've recently discovered about the world is:

Fri — What "experience" means to me:

> A MIND THAT IS STRETCHED BY A NEW EXPERIENCE CAN NEVER GO BACK TO ITS OLD DIMENSIONS.
>
> Oliver Wendell Holmes Jr., former US Supreme Court Justice

Sat — The best thing about learning something new is:

Sun — 3 new things I want to learn this year:

1 _____

2 _____

3 _____

Mon

Tue

Wed

Thu

Fri

Sat

Sun

A reflection on my week:

Mon To me, "integrity" means:

Tue I think before I speak because:

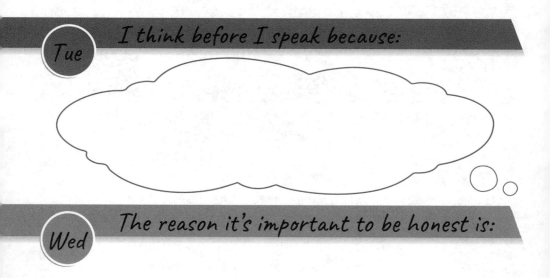

Wed The reason it's important to be honest is:

Thu I am inspired to change the world by:

Fri

If I have integrity, then I do not:

Sat

I show respect to others by:

> IF YOUR ACTIONS INSPIRE OTHERS TO DREAM MORE, LEARN MORE, DO MORE, AND BECOME MORE, YOU ARE A LEADER.
>
> *Author unknown*

Sun

Why it's important to be kind:

Mon I work hard at school because:

When faced with a challenge I tend to: **Tue**

Wed My biggest goal right now is:

To me, "believing in myself" means: **Thu**

I should never give up because: **Fri**

If I were president, I would: **Sat**

Sun I do my best when:

Mon

Being healthy means:

Tue

I can exercise my body by:

Wed

3 healthy habits I do every day:

- _____
- _____
- _____

Thu

I nurture my mind and body by:

> TO KEEP THE BODY IN GOOD HEALTH IS A DUTY...OTHERWISE WE SHALL NOT BE ABLE TO KEEP OUR MIND STRONG AND CLEAR.
>
> Gautama Buddha,
> religion founder

Fri My favorite healthy foods are:

Sat An unhealthy habit I am overcoming is
_____ because:

Sun I can relax my body by:

Month_____

Goals

	Monday	Tuesday	Wednesday

_____

_____

_____

_____

_____

Notes

_____

_____

_____

_____

_____

_____

Year

Thursday	Friday	Saturday	Sunday

Mon My most useful talent is:

The talent I am most grateful for is: **Tue**

 Wed I am really good at:

One skill I want to master is: **Thu**

 Fri The best quality about me is:

When I want to feel more confident, I: **Sat**

Sun The best thing to do on a rainy day is:

Mon   The colors I see outside today are:

Tue   When I am outside, the senses I am most thankful for are:

Wed   My favorite place to explore outdoors is _____ because:

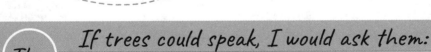

Thu   If trees could speak, I would ask them:

Fri I went outdoors and here's a drawing of what I saw:

 Sat The most beautiful place I have ever been is:

 Sun If I could teleport anywhere right now I'd go to _____ because:

> I BELIEVE THE WORLD IS INCOMPREHENSIBLY BEAUTIFUL — AN ENDLESS PROSPECT OF MAGIC AND WONDER.
>
> *Ansel Adams, American photographer*

Mon The craziest thing I ever ate was:

Tue If I could invent a fidget, it would be:

> **NOT THE SENSES I HAVE BUT WHAT I DO WITH THEM IS MY KINGDOM.**
>
> *Helen Keller, American author and disability rights advocate*

Wed When I stop and listen right now, I hear these sounds:

Thu My favorite toy to play with is:

70

Fri

My favorite smell is _____.
It reminds me of:

Sat

My favorite meal is:

Sun

3 things I appreciate about the sunshine:

- _____
- _____
- _____

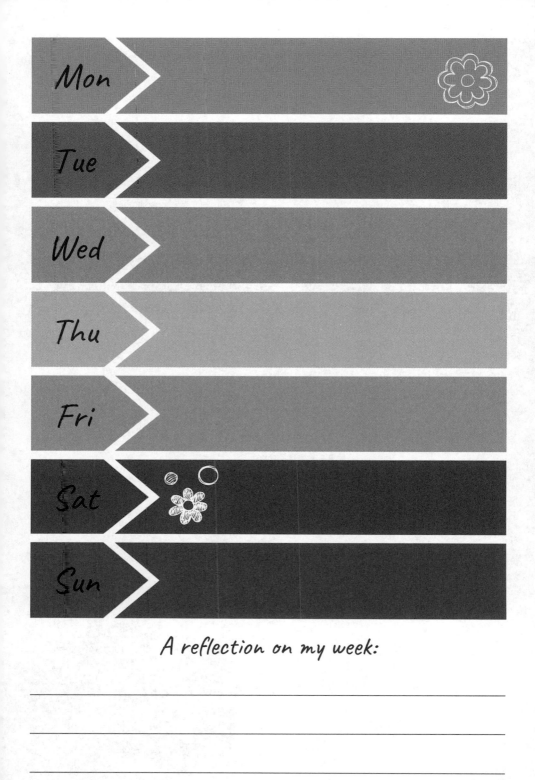

Mon

Tue

Wed

Thu

Fri

Sat

Sun

A reflection on my week:

_____

_____

_____

Mon What kindness means to me:

Tue Today I showed kindness to someone else by:

Wed I practice being kind to myself by:

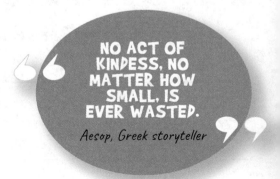

NO ACT OF KINDESS, NO MATTER HOW SMALL, IS EVER WASTED.

Aesop, Greek storyteller

74

Thu

When I do kind things for others, I feel:

Fri

3 people in my life who are kind to me:

1 _____

2 _____

3 _____

Sat

I spread kindness in my school by:

Sun

I could donate these things to help other kids in need:

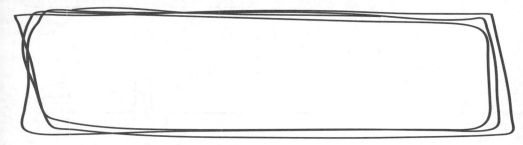

Month _____

Goals	Monday	Tuesday	Wednesday

Goals

_____

_____

_____

_____

_____

Notes

_____

_____

_____

_____

_____

_____

Year _____

Thursday	Friday	Saturday	Sunday

Mon

I am thankful I have:

> LET US BE GRATEFUL TO PEOPLE WHO MAKE US HAPPY; THEY ARE THE CHARMING GARDENERS WHO MAKE OUR SOULS BLOSSOM.
>
> *Marcel Proust,*
> *French novelist*

Tue

I appreciate my school because:

Wed

One possession that makes my life easier:

Thu I feel safe when:

Fri During free time I appreciate being able to:

Sat If I was given a piece of clay, I would create:

Sun 3 people I appreciate right now:

1 _____

2 _____

3 _____

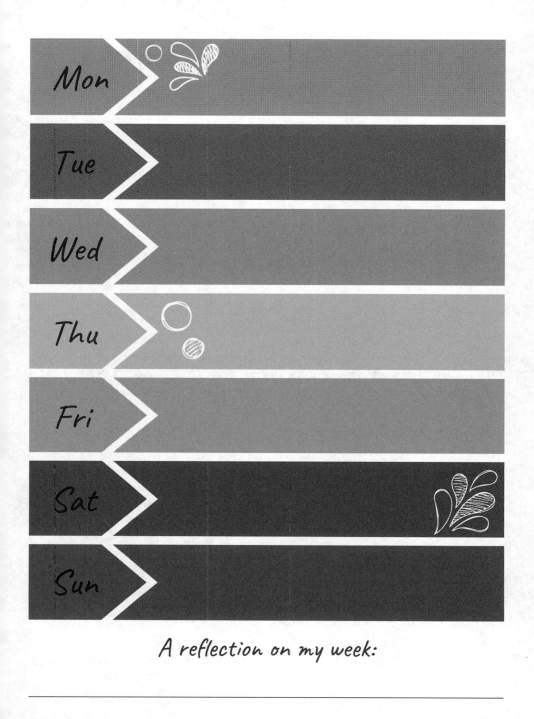

Mon

Tue

Wed

Thu

Fri

Sat

Sun

A reflection on my week:

_____

_____

_____

Mon Here is a drawing of how I feel when I know I'm being heard:

Tue I know when someone is listening when:

> THE NOBLEST PLEASURE IS THE JOY OF UNDERSTANDING.
>
> Leonardo da Vinci,
> Italian polymath

Wed A good listener is someone who:

Thu I am a good listener because:

Fri 3 things I will do today to be a better listener:

1 _____

2 _____

3 _____

Sat It's important to not interrupt others because:

Sun One thing I do to focus when someone is talking to me:

Mon I started my day by:

 Tue Sometimes I get distracted when:

 Wed A simple pleasure I'm thankful for:

 Thu When given a hard assignment, I:

 Fri If I knew I could not fail, I would:

 Sat I feel courageous when I:

 Sun I can practice patience by:

Mon Things I've done that I thought I could never do:

Tue When I feel stressed, I calm myself by:

Wed I feel comforted when:

Thu Here is a drawing of what surrounds me right now:

Fri My to-do list for relaxing tomorrow is:

> **THERE IS A CALMNESS TO A LIFE LIVED IN GRATITUDE, A QUIET JOY.**
>
> *Ralph H. Blum, American writer and cultural anthropologist*

Sat The place that makes me feel most peaceful is _____. If I were to describe that place using all five senses:

👁 Sight:

👂 Hearing:

✋ Taste:

👅 Touch:

👃 Smell:

Sun Today I will enjoy nature by:

Month_____

Goals

Monday	Tuesday	Wednesday

Notes

Year _____

Thursday	Friday	Saturday	Sunday

Mon My favorite costume ever is _____ because it makes me feel:

Tue If I wrote a book, the main character would be _____ and the story would be about:

IMAGINATION IS MORE IMPORTANT THAN KNOWLEDGE.

Albert Einstein, German theoretical physicist

Wed If I could be an animal, I would be a _____ because:

Thu Changes I'm noticing in the world around me:

Fri If I could make one wish come true for a day, it would be:

 Sat If I could have a superpower, it would be

_____ because:

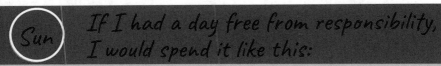 **Sun** If I had a day free from responsibility, I would spend it like this:

Mon 2 things I did today to strengthen my mind:

1 _____

2 _____

Tue My favorite activity that makes me feel strong is:

Wed One time I stood up for someone or something that was right:

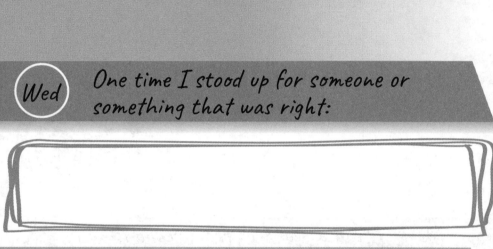

Thu If I witness an action that goes against my values, something I can do to stand against it is:

Fri Today I stepped outside of my comfort zone by:

Sat Something positive I can say to myself when I feel fear is:

Sun Here's a drawing of what being strong looks like to me:

I AM STRONGER THAN FEAR.

Malala Yousafzai, Pakistani activist

93

Mon I feel most brave when:

I feel strong when: **Tue**

 Wed One mistake that I learned from was:

My greatest strength is: **Thu**

Fri 2 things I am not afraid of:

1 _____

2 _____

My motto is: **Sat**

 Sun The bravest thing I've ever done is:

Mon Places I enjoy visiting:

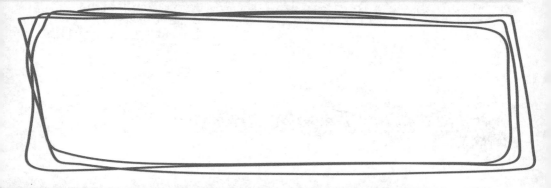

> CLIMB THE MOUNTAIN, NOT SO THE WORLD CAN SEE YOU, BUT SO YOU CAN SEE THE WORLD.
>
> *David McCullough Jr., American educator*

Tue When I was little, my favorite place to visit was:

Wed If I could live anywhere in the world, I would choose:

Thu My dream vacation is:

 Fri To me, the perfect weekend looks like:

 Sat When preparing for my dream vacation, I must pack:

 Sun If I were traveling the world, I would take _____ because:

Mon

Tue

Wed

Thu

Fri

Sat

Sun

A reflection on my week:

Month_____

Goals

Monday	Tuesday	Wednesday

_____

_____

_____

_____

_____

Notes

_____

_____

_____

_____

_____

_____

Year _____

Thursday	Friday	Saturday	Sunday

Mon My favorite song is _____ because:

Tue My favorite thing to do during free time is:

Wed My favorite food is _____ because:

Thu My favorite movie is _____ because:

102

Fri

My 3 favorite book characters are:

- _____
- _____
- _____

Sat

My favorite subject in school is
_____ because:

ALWAYS
BE ON THE
LOOKOUT FOR
THE PRESENCE
OF WONDER.

E. B. White,
American writer

Sun

My favorite teacher ever is _____
because:

Mon To love myself means:

I deserve to be happy because: **Tue**

 Wed My closest friend is _____ because:

I know that I am loved because: **Thu**

Fri I feel loved when:

Someone who shows me love every day: **Sat**

 Sun Today I will make this a great day by:

Mon Today I laughed about:

 Tue The funniest thing I have ever seen:

 Wed My most embarrassing moment that I can laugh about now is:

 Thu If I had a pet sloth, I would:

Fri   My favorite joke:

Sat   The funniest sounding word I've heard is:

Sun   The funniest person I know is _____ because:

Mon A challenge I overcame this week:

My favorite thing about my personality is: **Tue**

Wed When I make a mistake, I feel:

My best friend would describe me as: **Thu**

Fri One thing I strongly disliked but like now is:

In order to learn, I must: **Sat**

 Sun I am most proud of:

Mon To me, "leadership" is:

Tue A time I spoke up for something I believed in:

> FIGHT FOR THE THINGS THAT YOU CARE ABOUT, BUT DO IT IN A WAY THAT WILL LEAD OTHERS TO JOIN YOU.
>
> *Ruth Bader Ginsburg, former US Supreme Court Justice*

Wed Someone I admire with strong values is _____, because:

Thu How it feels when someone stands up for me:

Fri Three values that are important to me:

1 _____

2 _____

3 _____

Sat If I see someone being bullied, I:

Sun When a classmate is struggling with something, I:

Month_____

Goals

Monday	Tuesday	Wednesday

Notes

Year _____

Thursday	Friday	Saturday	Sunday

Mon

What "compassion" means to me:

Tue

The most compassionate person I know is:

Wed

3 things I can do to encourage others this week:

1 _____

2 _____

3 _____

Thu

Some things I love about the people in my life are:

Fri It's important to not gossip because:

Sat One place I would like to volunteer my time to help others:

IF YOU SEE SOMEONE WITHOUT A SMILE, GIVE THEM YOURS.

Dolly Parton, American singer-songwriter

Sun This week I will practice kindness by:

Mon If I could invent something, it would be:

My favorite art activity is: **Tue**

Wed Creativity has helped me:

My creative strengths are: **Thu**

Fri If I had the power to change one thing in school, I would change:

3 things I enjoy doing: **Sat**

1 _____

2 _____

3 _____

I appreciate where I live because:
Sun

Mon Someone who I look up to:

Tue My hopes and dreams are:

Wed The year is 2035 and my dream life looks like this:

Thu 3 ways I am different now from the beginning of the year:

- _____
- _____
- _____

Fri Here is a drawing of me in the future working at my dream job:

Sat Today I will create a goal poster and will include these 3 things:

1 _____

2 _____

3 _____

Sun I want to change the world by:

Mon To me, "confidence" means:

WITH CONFIDENCE, YOU HAVE WON BEFORE YOU HAVE STARTED.

Marcus Garvey,
Jamaican activist

Tue Today, I'll practice loving myself by:

Wed 3 things I like about myself:

- _____
- _____
- _____

Thu When I look in the mirror, I see:

Fri An opportunity my school has given me to learn something new is:

Sat My hero is _____. Some challenges this person has overcome to be their best self are:

Sun The most challenging goal I've achieved is:

121

Mon

Tue

Wed

Thu

Fri

Sat

Sun

A reflection on my week:

_____

_____

_____

Month _____

Goals

_____

_____

_____

_____

_____

Notes

_____

_____

_____

_____

Monday	Tuesday	Wednesday

Year_____

Thursday	Friday	Saturday	Sunday

Mon

3 things that bring me joy:

1 _____

2 _____

3 _____

Tue

The most talented person I know is

_____ because:

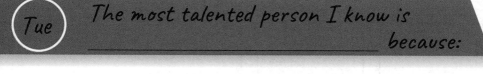

Wed

One of my favorite days ever was:

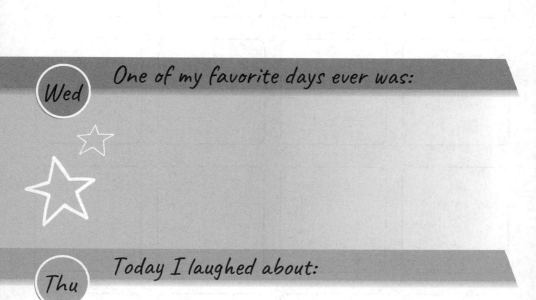

Thu

Today I laughed about:

Fri — Today I am thankful that:

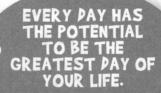

> **EVERY DAY HAS THE POTENTIAL TO BE THE GREATEST DAY OF YOUR LIFE.**
>
> *Lin-Manuel Miranda, American actor and playwright*

Sat — This week I noticed these beautiful things:

Sun — I can bring joy to others by:

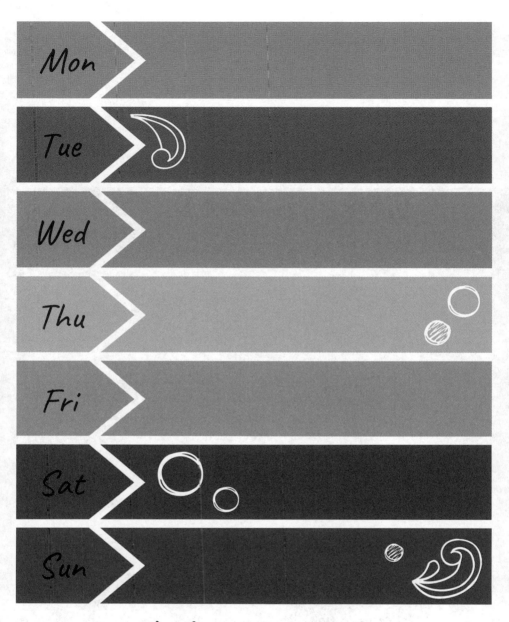

Mon

Tue

Wed

Thu

Fri

Sat

Sun

A reflection on my week:

_____

_____

_____

Mon To me, "home" means:

Tue My favorite spot in my home is
_____ because:

Wed If someone opens my desk drawer, they will find:

Thu If I could build my dream house, it would be:

Fri

3 things I can't go without in my home:

1 _____

2 _____

3 _____

Sat

I feel most comfortable when:

Sun

My favorite memory of my home is:

HOME IS WHERE ONE STARTS FROM.

T. S. Eliot,
American poet

Mon When I grow up I want to be:

Tue My #1 goal is:

 Wed If I could travel back in time, I would want to meet:

When I daydream, I often think about: **Thu**

 Fri I was inspired by my teacher when:

My teacher always tells me: **Sat**

 Sun I feel most confident and capable when:

Mon I choose to be honest about my feelings because:

Tue What being trustworthy means to me:

Wed Keeping promises means:

Thu The people in my life I trust:

Fri

I stick up for my friends and family by:

> ALWAYS STAND ON PRINCIPLE, EVEN IF YOU STAND ALONE.
>
> *John Adams, second US President*

Sat

Telling the truth is important because:

Sun

I show myself compassion and kindness by doing these things:

135

Month _____

Goals

_____

_____

_____

_____

_____

	Monday	Tuesday	Wednesday

Notes

_____

_____

_____

_____

_____

Year _____

Thursday	Friday	Saturday	Sunday

Mon To me "diversity" means:

Tue The best part about spending time with people who are different from me is:

Wed Our differences make the world more interesting and better because:

Thu Something I can do at my school to cultivate inclusion is:

Fri A time I made someone feel accepted and appreciated:

 Sat A culture I would like to learn more about is _____ because:

WE ARE ALL DIFFERENT AND THAT'S BEAUTIFUL.

Karen Salmansohn, American author

 Sun It's important to learn from people that are different from me because:

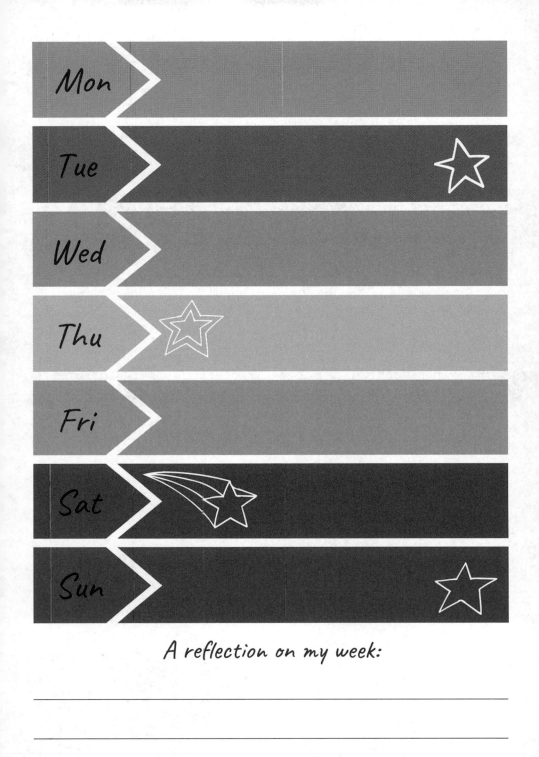

Mon

Tue

Wed

Thu

Fri

Sat

Sun

A reflection on my week:

_____

_____

_____

Mon I feel different from others when I:

 Tue A historical figure I've always wanted to learn more about is _____ because:

 Wed It's OK to have different ideas, because:

Thu Diversity is important to me because:

THE RICHEST PEOPLE IN LIFE ARE THE GOOD LISTENERS.

Stephen Graham, British author

Fri My opinion matters because:

Sat If I notice someone who has trouble making friends, I can help by:

Sun I am very different from my parents because:

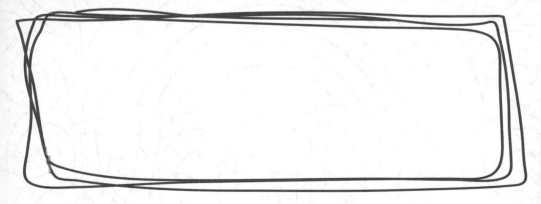

Mon So far, my favorite thing about this day is:

A pep talk I can give myself when
I'm struggling: **Tue**

Wed How can courage lead to new ideas?

The most courageous person I know is: **Thu**

Things that scare me:
Fri

How I overcome become scared: **Sat**

I helped someone be courageous when I:
 Sun

Mon — My favorite song is _____ because:

Tue — If I were a professional singer, I would sing about:

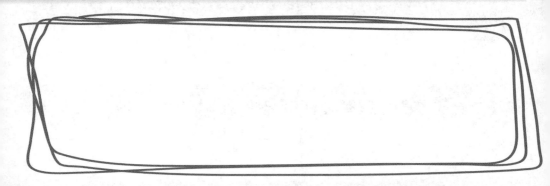

Wed — My earliest memory of music is:

MUSIC IS LIFE ITSELF.

Louis Armstrong, American musician and entertainer

146

Thu My favorite playlist includes:

Fri The music I listen to with my friends:

Sat My favorite song lyrics that make me happy:

Sun If I could master one musical instrument, it would be _____ because:

Month_____

Goals

Monday	Tuesday	Wednesday

Notes

_____

Year _____

Thursday	Friday	Saturday	Sunday

Mon

I feel happiest when:

Tue

3 things that give me positive energy:

1 _____

2 _____

3 _____

Wed

Listening to music makes me feel:

Thu

I make others happy by:

Fri

Right now I'm feeling:

Sat

My happiest memory of the last year is:

Sun

Some sayings that make me feel good:

Mon One way I deal with disappointment in a positive way is:

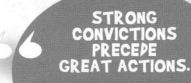

STRONG CONVICTIONS PRECEDE GREAT ACTIONS.

James Freeman Clarke, American author and human rights advocate

Tue It's important to always be myself because:

Wed I turn setbacks into opportunities by:

Thu

One time I overcame an obstacle and it made me stronger:

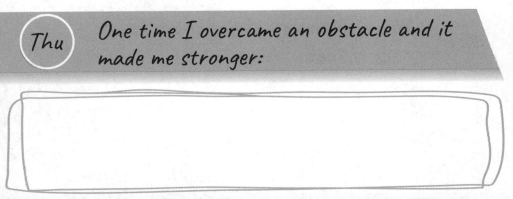

Fri

If I had all the courage in the world to try something, I would:

Sat

A challenge I have recently overcome is:

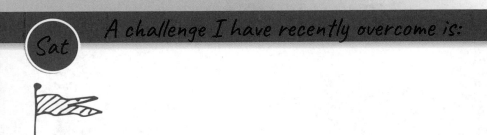

Sun

The most important thing to me in overcoming adversity is:

Mon When someone recognizes my hard work, I feel:

Tue It's easy for me to work hard on these 2 things:

1 _____

2 _____

Wed My greatest success has been:

Thu I am most proud of:

Fri When I feel discouraged, I can turn it around by telling myself:

 Sat When I earn good grades, I feel:

Sun When I practice a skill and get better at it, I feel:

SUCCESS IS NOT SOMETHING TO WAIT FOR, IT IS SOMETHING TO WORK FOR.

Henry Wadsworth Longfellow, American poet

A positive attitude feels like:

Tue

3 things I love about myself:

1 _____

2 _____

3 _____

Wed

I love myself because:

Thu

I believe in myself because I know:

Fri One thing I've learned about myself this year is:

Sat My favorite positive words are:

" FOR THERE IS ALWAYS LIGHT, IF ONLY WE'RE BRAVE ENOUGH TO SEE IT. IF ONLY WE'RE BRAVE ENOUGH TO BE IT. "

Amanda Gorman, American poet

Sun I am brave because:

1 _____
2 _____
3 _____
4 _____
5 _____

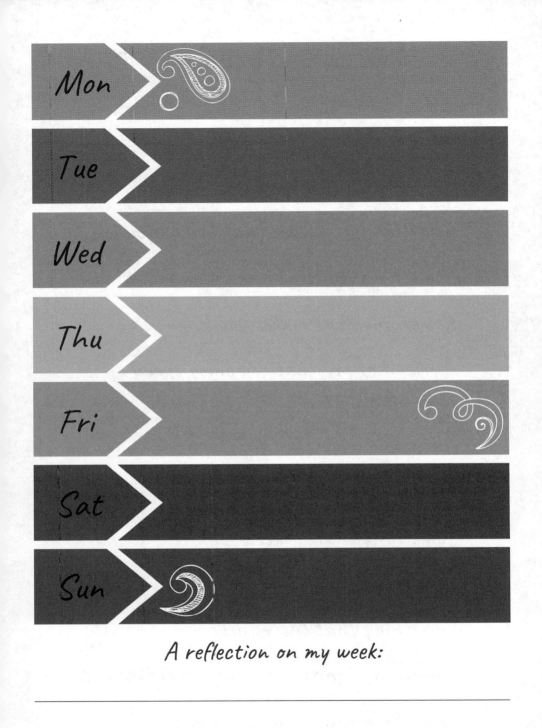

Mon

Tue

Wed

Thu

Fri

Sat

Sun

A reflection on my week:

_____

_____

_____

Can you find them all?

- [ ] Something in nature that brings you joy.
- [ ] Something that will make someone else smile.
- [ ] Something that makes you laugh.
- [ ] A friend or pet that you enjoy spending time with.
- [ ] Something soft or fluffy.
- [ ] A picture that brings back good memories.
- [ ] Something that makes a beautiful sound.
- [ ] Something that you enjoy doing outside.
- [ ] Something that tastes delicious.
- [ ] Something that you can use to create art.
- [ ] Something that is useful to you.
- [ ] Something you love doing with your friends.

GRATITUDE SCAVENGER HUNT

- [ ] Someone you can help today.

- [ ] Something from nature that is your favorite color.

- [ ] Something in your home that makes you smile.

- [ ] A favorite book that you are thankful for.

- [ ] Your favorite smell.

- [ ] A special quiet place where you can write & retreat.

- [ ] Something that you are very proud of.

- [ ] A picture or drawing that makes you feel calm.

- [ ] A favorite note that someone has written to you.

- [ ] Something that reminds you of how loved you are.

- [ ] Something that you would like to share with others.

Notes

Notes

Notes

About the Author

Cameon Galli has been reflecting and doodling in journals since she was a young girl. This lifelong practice of self-discovery became the cornerstone for a routine designed around being present and mindful. She is passionate about helping children cultivate confidence while nurturing their creativity. She uses relatable content to help children establish healthy habits that encourage them in the art of finding gratitude and joy, even during times of struggle.

Cameon resides in northern Illinois with her husband, two daughters, and big baby Reuther (their 180-pound English mastiff). When not working her dream job, you'll find her on the sidelines of a soccer field, creating and crafting with her children, gardening, reading, and spending time with family and friends.

About the Designers

Kim Balacuit is an illustrator and designer living in sunny Florida. She has previously worked with Sesame Street and Abrams Books making content she cares about for kids. When she's not buried in artwork, you can find her reading at the beach, practicing (and failing) at roller skating, daydreaming about dogs, or finding the spiciest foods to eat. You can visit her work at www.kimbalacuit.com.

Lilia Garvin is an illustrator and designer living in Texas with her amazing wife Georgia, their two active dogs, and several adorable rats. Outside of designing books, she can be found playing D&D, baking savory pies, exploring dog parks, and expressing her love for painting in all shapes: watercolor, oil, acrylic, digital, and more. You can visit her work at LiliaGarvin.com

Woo! Jr. Kids Activities is passionate about inspiring children to learn through imagination and FUN. That is why we have provided thousands of craft ideas, printables, and teacher resources to over 55 million people since 2008. We are on a mission to produce books that allow kids to build knowledge, express their talent, and grow into creative, compassionate human beings. Elementary education teachers, day care professionals, and parents have come to rely on Woo! Jr. for high-quality, engaging, and innovative content that children LOVE. Our bestselling kids activity books have sold over 300,000 copies worldwide.

Tap into our free kids activity ideas at our website WooJr.com or by following us on social media:

 https://www.pinterest.com/woojrkids/
 https://www.facebook.com/WooJr/
 https://twitter.com/woojrkids
 https://www.instagram.com/woojrkids/

DragonFruit, an imprint of Mango Publishing, publishes high-quality children's books to inspire a love of lifelong learning in readers. DragonFruit publishes a variety of titles for kids, including children's picture books, nonfiction series, toddler activity books, pre-K activity books, science and education titles, and ABC books. Beautiful and engaging, our books celebrate diversity, spark curiosity, and capture the imaginations of parents and children alike.

Mango Publishing, established in 2014, publishes an eclectic list of books by diverse authors. We were named the Fastest Growing Independent Publisher by Publishers Weekly in 2019 and 2020. Our success is bolstered by our main goal, which is to publish high-quality books that will make a positive impact in people's lives.

Our readers are our most important resource; we value your input, suggestions, and ideas. We'd love to hear from you—after all, we are publishing books for you!

Please stay in touch with us and follow us at:
Instagram: @dragonfruitkids
Facebook: Mango Publishing
Twitter: @MangoPublishing
LinkedIn: Mango Publishing
Pinterest: Mango Publishing

Sign up for our newsletter at www.mangopublishinggroup.com and receive a free book! Join us on Mango's journey to change publishing, one book at a time.